STATE FINANCES.

A VINDICATION

OF THE

MANAGEMENT OF THE STATE FINANCES,

BY THE

REPUBLICAN ADMINISTRATION,

BEING

A REPLY TO THE "MINORITY REPORT" OF THE SPECIAL COMMITTEE UPON STATE AFFAIRS, SUBMITTED AT THE EXTRA SESSION OF THE LEGISLATURE, JAN., 1858.

By Chas. V. DeLand.

LANSING:
PRINTED AT THE REPUBLICAN OFFICE.
1858.

STATE FINANCES.

There are times when it is eminently proper for Legislative bodies to make investigations into the affairs of States and Nations, and by a thorough, careful and truthful review of history, by close applications of reasoning as to causes and effects, by making honorable and truthful contrasts, arrive at, and open to the public view the sources of the State or National prosperity, or the causes of its financial, governmental and political derangement and embarrassments. When properly, wisely and honestly conducted, investigations of this character always redound to the public good, but when confined within the limits of a narrow and selfish partizanship—when the Statesman and Legislator is sunk below the level of the demagogue and political trickster—when the reporter divests himself of political responsibility and personal individuality and lends himself to the base and dishonest machinations of corrupt and libelous associates—when the report itself, is perverted from the legitimate character of a State paper to that of a falsifying and malicious attack upon personal honesty and integrity—*such investigations* are useful only as an exhibition of the want of character, moral and political integrity of the men who engage in their preparation, the servility of their party feelings and political principles, and the desperate and hopeless chances of their political success.

To say that the document denominated a "Report" by the minority of the Special Committee of Investigation into the Financial Affairs of the State, authorized by the House, at the late Extra Session of our State Legislature, and signed by "E. Kanter," as one of the Committee, bears in all its features these characteristics, and is amenable in all its parts to such reflections, is simply reiterating to all who have heard or read that "Report," a patent truth. To dignify it with any other title than an "*electioneering splurge*," would be to pervert its character and subject it to merited ridicule. To call it *a history* of the financial affairs or condition of the State, would be giving currency to an absurd and foolish falsehood.

It may be proper, in this connection, to refer to the authors of this remarkable "report," vouched for by "undersigned" as "one of the committee." Enough is known of it to establish its paternity with such men as the notorious Dr. Alvord, the equally notorious and more unscrupulous Thompson, of the Grand Rapids *Enquirer*, Griswold, the ostensible editor of the Lansing *Journal*, and others of that ilk, the whole being under the immediate supervision and direction of the Hon. George W. Peck. The mere mention of this corps of authors and politicans is a conclusive answer to the "report" where the authors are known; but lest there might be some misunderstanding, and some few honest men really think it was the production of "the undersigned," it is proper to thus state its parentage, before reviewing some of the statements of the "report" itself.

The opening paragraph of the "report" sets forth with doleful lugubriousness the great disadvantages which beset "the undersigned" and his associates in their arduous pursuit of knowledge under great difficulties. They state, though not in words, that they were denied all information from the State departments, and were compelled to rely upon unauthenticated reports, AND THEIR OWN RESOURCES! This insinuation is palpably false, as they were afforded the same aid and figures which were asked and furnished to the majority. It is true the minority of the Committee made requests of the Chairman of the Committee as well as the State Treasurer for privileges and information upon certain matters entirely without the scope of the resolution demanding the investigation, and which had not the most remote bearing upon the subject matter referred to the Committee, and of which there was no shadow of necessity; which requests were, of course, and properly, refused; and upon this refusal to gratify a paltry spirit of personal malignity, and a prompt repulsion of insolent imputation, by the State Treasurer, is founded the lacrymore sympathy of the "undersigned"—the wail for sympathy with which the "report" is opened. When it says the "undersigned was obliged to go into the investigation single-handed," we are prone to believe the truth of the statement in consideration of the weakness of *the thing;* but seriously protest against the attempt of "the undersigned" to rob his associates, before mentioned, of their due proportion of the laurels to be reaped among the "unterrified," in the compilation of the "report."

"The undersigned" in opening his review of the finances of the State, commences with the assertion that in the year

1848, "there was in the Treasury the sum of $62,304 45, which sum was increased in 1854 to half a million of dollars." In this connection "the undersigned" omits a very important link in the history of the State. He is perfectly oblivious as to the source from which this surplus was obtained, and gives no explanation whether it was a *bona fide* surplus, or simply a balance of borrowed money, on hand, kept on hand by a process of "shinning" adopted in the early history of the State by his party, and which would do credit to the most experienced street operator in New York or Boston. Had "the undersigned" been disposed to meet the issue fairly, he would not have omitted such an important link, but would have stated the fact that this money was all borrowed, and its appearance in the State Treasury was only an evidence of indebtedness of the State to that amount. It is a well known fact that the State has but one fund—"the general fund"—and that this fund is and has been *bankrupt* for the past twenty years. Upon this point the report of the majority well says:

"Another source of the large surplus in the Treasury, was the system adopted in relation to our *Trust Funds*, by which the principal was loaned to the State as fast as received, and used for the payment of current expenses or outstanding liabilities."

And it is evident at first sight that a balance of that character, and so obtained, instead of being an evidence of State prosperity and financial strength, is a direct admission and an unanswerable argument to the contrary. A careful search into *the facts* would have revealed to "the undersigned" this truth—that in addition to the enormous debt entailed upon the State by the recklessness and extravagance of the Democratic party, amounting, in 1854, to over two millions of dollars, the State, under this Democratic policy, had also borrowed from other sources, to pay its current expenses, the snug little sum of eight hundred thousand dollars. Now, granting all that "the undersigned" claims when he says the Republicans found this surplus of over half a million in the State Treasury, to be true, did not common justice and candor call upon him to acknowledge that it was, like all other "Democratic" thunder, "*borrowed capital*"—a fund upon which the State was compelled to pay an enormous interest, the lowest rates being seven per cent. per annum—thus making, as every intelligent man may see at a glance, this boasted surplus, really and practically a direct tax upon the people to the amount of the interest, while the money was lying idle in the Treasury, useful only in an electioneering extremity—an idle boast that there was "plenty of cash in the State Treasury." A like policy pursued in the transaction of individual business, would subject the person pursuing it to serious imputations, and such an explanation to creditors or the public by a business man, coupled with the claim that his borrowed money should be reckoned as a portion of his *bona fide* capital or assets, available to his general credits, would inspire serious doubts either of honesty or sanity, and perhaps of both.

It is plain, then, that although the Democrats left a surplus in the Treasury, it was only a fictitious surplus—a surplus, each dollar of which added really a large per centage to the actual indebtedness of the State. The sum thus borrowed from the Trust Funds by the State was, as before stated, about eight hundred thousand dollars, of the principal of which near three hundred thousand dollars had been expended to pay the *ordinary expenses of the State government*, leaving a surplus of about five hundred thousand dollars. We have asserted that this surplus, instead of being an advantage to the State, was a detriment. To prove this, we have only to append a short statement of the receipts and expenditures of these Trust Funds for the past six years. It will be proper to remark for a full understanding of the table, that the basis upon which the loaning of these Trust Funds were established, carried with it the credits or profits of the funds, which also serves largely to increase the expenditures of the State, and adds each years' accumulating interest to the total of the sums thus loaned. It appears from the figures submitted by the majority of the committee that this species of the State indebtedness is increasing with astonishing rapidity, and it would be an absolute injustice to the Democratic party and "the undersigned," did we omit to expose this peculiarly beneficial result of their financial economy, entailed upon the State in the loaning of their Trust Funds.

The following table exhibits the receipts for interests, forfeitures, &c., on the entire proceeds of the borrowed funds which accrued to their credit during each year for the last six years, also, the interest which the State pays for the use of these Funds for the same period:

YEARS	Receipts.	Expenditures.
1852,........................	$50,113 31	$ 71,706 40
1853,........................	56,271 65	73,353 89
1854,........................	59,889 51	120,383 31

Total expenditures,..................	$255,443 60
Total receipts,......................	166,274 47
Excess of expenditures over receipts,..	$ 89,169 13

1855,........................	$77,666 75	$127,542 61
1856,........................	83,333 05	146,542 26
1857,........................	88,049 16	153,011 20

Total expenditures,..................	$427,096 07
Total receipts,......................	249,048 66
Excess of expenditures over receipts,..	$178,047 11
Excess of Democratic years,..........	89,169 13
	$267,216 24

Thus it will be seen that upon this item alone during the last six years, this "shinning" policy of the Democratic party has cost the State *a direct loss* of $267,216 24, or an average of $44,534 83 per annum of actual increased indebtedness upon the interest account of the Trust Funds alone!! By adding this *loss* on the interest fund to the principal of the Trust Funds borrowed and expended, it will be seen that this species of indebtedness entailed "in pursuance of the wise and economical policy of Governors Barry and Felch," has burdened the people of the State with a debt of *over one million two hundred thousand dollars*, in addition to the balance of *two millions* and over due upon the five million loan—thus making the *bona fide* indebtedness of the State something *over three millions of dollars*, all directly traceable to and chargable upon the reckless, short-sighted and extraordinary financial policy of this Democratic party. Is it any wonder that "the undersigned" is so totally oblivious to the real facts of our financial history, and slurs over all this important and instructive portion with the bland and flattering remark that when the Democratic party went out of power, they "left a large surplus in the Treasury?" But did they not also leave a *surplus of debts*, and a never-ending legacy of accumulating interest, which the people will soon be called upon to pay in the shape of a direct tax, which overshadows that little *surplus*, as the towering Himmalayan peak overshadows the diminutive mole-hills at their base.

But we pass on to that portion of the "report" which alludes to the expenditures of the State Government. "The undersigned" says:

"The expenditures during those seven years of the Democratic administration were annually from $371,491 47, the lowest, in 1848, to $449,355 40, the largest, in 1850."

And here we ask careful attention to the figures of "the undersigned," and those we shall quote. The "Report" says that in 1848, *the lowest year of Democratic rule*, the expenditures were only $371,491 47, while the official report of the State Treasurer for that year shows the expenditures to have been $404,426 35—evidently showing a mistake in "the undersigned" of $32,934 88. The "report" also says that in 1850, the largest year of Democratic rule, the expenditures were $449,355 40, while the official figures are $449,451 54, showing a mistake of "the undersigned" to the small sum of $106 14. We adduce the figures and make the corrections, not because they are necessary to the argument we intend to pursue on this head, but simply to show how little "the undersigned" knows about arithmetic, and how utterly incompetent such Democrats are to make a fair, liberal and honest investigation, or even to tell the truth.

Much ado is made by "the undersigned" in his "report" about the increased expenditures of the three years of Republican rule,.over the last three years of Democratic rule of the State. "The undersigned" estimates this excess as follows:

Rep. years.		Dem. years.	Excess.
1855	over	1852,	$175,432 48
1856	"	1853,	190,523 66
1857	"	1854,	230,623 79
Total excess,			$596,569 93

Were these figures true, we should be well pleased to let them stand as they are, but we would not deal unjustly, even with "the undersigned," and hence, though probably unfortunate for the Republican party, we will correct the misstatements of the minority "report," by giving the following *official* figures for the expenditures of the six years mentioned:

Years	Dem. expenditures.	Years.	Rep. expenditures.	Rep excess.
1852,....	$421,918 97	1855,....	$624,777 88	$260,858 91
1853,....	396,449 39	1856,....	639,879 06	243,430 67
1854,....	433,469 57	1857,....	679,976 19	246,509 62
	1,251,837 93		1,944,636 13	692,799 20
Estimated excess of "the undersigned,"....				596,569 93
In which "the undersigned" falls short,....				$96,229 27

In this connection it is proper for us to note the extraordinary expenses which have been made during the last three years, over and above the expenditures of the like character for the three preceding years of Democratic rule, which we present in the following table:

Excess of Expenditures for 1855, '56 *and* '57, *over the years* 1852, '53 *and* '54, *for the same items, as follows:*

Interest on State debt, funded,..............	$ 88,377 62
Interest on Trust Funds loaned by the State,.	88,877 98
Paid on State debt,........................	147,035 34
Compilation of the Laws,..................	24,874 08
Building bridges and other improvements at Lansing, authorized by acts of Legislature,.	15,159 96
Excess of appropriations to public works in 1855, '56 and '57, over same objects for 1852, '53 and '54,..........................	314,175 31
Allowances of Democratic Board of Auditors and expenses of State government in Dec. 1854, charged to fiscal year of 1855,........	83,962 71
	$762,463 00
Total excess of expenditures for 1855, '56 and '57, over those of 1852, '53 and '54,........	692,799 20
Showing a decrease in the actual current expenses of the State government in the last 3 years over the preceding 3 years of......	$69,674 80

Being an actual saving to the people, in the current expenses of each of the three years of Republican administration of TWENTY-THREE THOUSAND TWO HUNDRED AND TWENTY-FOUR DOLLARS AND NINETY-THREE CENTS!! ($23,224 93!)

To which should be added $60,000 of interest paid upon the surplus revenue by the Republican Administration, more than was paid during the seven years of Democratic rule; and you have an annual gain and saving to the State under Republican rule of $43,324 93, or $129,074 80 for the three years of Republican rule saved in the ordinary expenses of the government.

It greatly behooves the anxious gentlemen who compiled that "report" to prate about economy, when a plain and fair showing of the figures indicate that "had the same system of economy existed in the expenditures of the general fund," under the Democratic administrations that *has* existed and *been practiced* by the present Republican Administration, the State would have been saved its entire indebtedness, and the people now have been entirely free from taxation.

In regard to the items mentioned in the above table, it is proper to remark that they were mainly of that necessary and unavoidable character which forbade the interposition of any plea of policy or political consideration. The credit and standing of the State at home and abroad required the payment of the Bonds and the interest, while the appropriations for the State Asylums, Prison, Normal School, &c., were equally necessary to the prosperity, efficiency and maintenance of those institutions. But we shall speak more particularly of these subjects in another place.

And now we come to the veritable "mare's nest" of the "report," and it is truly a wonderful discovery! "The undersigned" and his associates open their eyes wide with well-feigned astonishment, when they found that the expenses of the State for printing, paper, &c., in the last three years, are increased, somewhat, over those items for previous years. Strange, indeed, when the business of every department has nearly doubled—some, as the Land Office and Superintendent of Public Instruction, quadrupled—that the expense for stationery and postage should increase in a like ratio! And in addition to this natural increase of business in the offices, the entire cost of the new compilation of the Laws of the State is charged into the current expenses of the last year. In "lumping" all these expenses together in this manner, "the undersigned" shows much more ingenuity than honesty, as it affords him an excellent opportunity to *double up* items with little fear of detection, (a sort of operation, Mr. Peck, most certainly, as the Auditor's Books show, was somewhat familiar with.) We do not intend, now, to answer all these little charges in detail, but shall take occasion in the future to contrast, item by item, all the expenses of the State under the present Administration with those of its predecessors. But to illustrate, we will give the totals of the bills for stationery for two years and see how they compare with each other.

The Democratic Board of Auditors allowed, in 1854, for stationery, gold pens, "super royal" at $28!! per ream, &c., for the use of the State Departments, the sum of.......................................$5,679 18

The Republican Board of Auditors allowed in 1857, for stationery, gold pens, super royal, at $26 per ream, &c., the sum of............... 4,176 91

Showing a saving by the Republican Administration, in 1857, over the Democratic allowances tor 1854, of.......................................$1,502 27

in the item of stationery alone, and this, too, notwithstanding the current business of the Government had *nearly doubled* in the intervening years. And a comparison of all the other expenses of the State offices, with the single exception, perhaps, of postage, would show the same relative saving to the State. Of course, as the current business and correspondence of the State Departments, inclusive with our natural growth of population, organization of new towns and counties, &c., the postage and stationery accounts should present a corresponding increase in their amounts. As to the "hundreds of reams of printing paper at $10 75 per ream," it is proper to say that this was used for the new compilation of laws, a work of over 1,700 pages, of which 10,000 copies were ordered printed.

The next point made in the "report," is in reference to "traveling expenses of State officers," "extra clerk hire," &c. Upon this point "the undersigned" says:

"A large increase, however, is experienced in the State Department in the payment of extra clerks, extra compensation to State officers, and traveling expenses of State officers and their clerks, by which, under the plea of 'on official business,' the Treasury has been pilfered to a large extent. The undersigned believes that, as those officers are liberally paid by the State for their services, it is the duty of the Board of State Auditors to scrutinize closely and thoroughly the character and correctness of such accounts before auditing the same, and to reject any claim of a dubious character."

In this connection, and to prove this bold assertion, however, the report omits all reference to figures. Perhaps this is well, as we have already shown the total incorrectness of every table or computation made by "the undersigned." But in this matter there were undoubtedly prudential motives for relying upon *assertions* and avoiding comparisons. We have taken the trouble to examine into this matter carefully, and present the following figures, compiled from the Reports of the State Auditors for 1854 and 1857, showing the relative economy of Democratic and Republican traveling expenses:

In 1854, the Democratic Board allowed to the different State officers, clerks, &c., for traveling expenses, $1,011 30
In 1857, the Republican Board allowed traveling expenses,.................................. 706 37

Showing a decline in such expenses of........ $304 43
instead of, as the "report" says, "a large increase of such expenses."

We also find by that report that the same Democratic Board of Auditors allowed to sundry individuals and as extra clerk hire, attorney fees, &c., for the single year of 1854, the sum of............................ $6,448 79
The Republican Board allowed, in 1857, (including $950, expenses in prosecuting the claim against the Phœnix Bank,) the sum of........ 2,775 38

Being a decrease in this class of expenditures for 1857, over the year 1854, of.................. $3,673 41
Add to this the above sum of................... 304 43

And we have a decrease in this class of expenses for 1857, over the year 1854, of.............. $3,977 84
instead of the "*large increase*," which "the undersigned" prates so flippantly about in his most absurd and untruthful "Minority Report." Will not the people reject with scorn the political tricksters and unscrupulous liars who attempt to deceive them with such statements.

One of the "notorious allowances" alluded to in the "report" of "the undersigned" is to Jonas H. Titus, for a journey to Pittsburg, of which he says:

"Upon information on the subject, I am convinced that the object of the journey was of a mere political character—that of attending the Republican Convention at Pittsburg—than the design of acquiring information in regard to the solitary cell system of the State Prison there."

When the reader is told that Mr. Titus made this journey nearly a year before the assembling of the Pittsburg

Convention, there will be no necessity of any further allusion to *this* matter. Another of the "extraordinary allowances" which "the undersigned" *digs up*, is one of $1,474 81 for fitting up the Legislative Hall for the use of the Legislature. The Democratic Board of Auditors in 1854, allowed $3,055 00, or $1,580 19 more than the Republicans paid for the same purpose, allowing the figures of the minority to be correct. And while speaking of this class of expenses, we would respectfully remind "the undersigned" that his party paid the snug little sum of $1,000 45 for carpets for the State offices, purchased chairs at $20 each, and paid $7 50 for cushions which could be purchased any where for from $2 50 to $3 00 each. We suppose it was no part of the intention of the "undersigned" to mention *these* little allowances, but as they are extremely pertitent in this conection we must be excused for introducing them.

The "report" next charges Hon. S. B. Treadwell with falsehood in paying Charles J. Harvey $150 00 for services as follows:

"By reference to a communication of Hon. S. B. Treadwell, the Commissioner of the State Land Office, published in the House Journal of 1857, dated February 11th, 1857, the undersigned learns that, notwithstanding the assurances of that gentleman that the State had assumed no liability and incurred no expense by the appointment of a tresspass agent for the Upper Peninsula, the sum of $150 has been paid to Mr. C. J. Harvey for services, and audited by the Board of State Auditors. The undersigned respectfully recommends an investigation of this affair.

We will save "the undersigned" the trouble of investigation by stating that although the sum mentioned was paid to Mr. Harvey, it was paid to him as an agent for other parties, as the vouchers will show, and not for services as timber agent; neither has Harvey or any other person (since the days of C. J. Fox,) been paid *out of the State Treasury*, for any such services.

The next paragraph of the "report" reads as follows:

"In the Annual Report of the Board of State Auditors of 1855, the undersigned finds a claim allowed for $408 80, to K. S. Bingham, Whitney Jones and Silas M. Holmes, for traveling expenses and attendance to Saut Ste Mary, which was a most injudicious and unwarranted disbursement of the public funds, as this expenditure was not based upon any Legislative act and authority.

We will not dispute the allowance of this sum to the

persons mentioned, nor the propriety of such allowance, but to show that this *was a judicious* and *warranted* "disbursement of the canal funds", and that the expenditure *was* based upon *a* "Legislative act and authority," we beg leave to refer "the undersigned" to act No. 91 of the Session Laws of 1855, sec. 4, which reads as follows:

"Sec. 4. It shall be the duty of said Board of Control to make from time to time, such rules and regalations as they may deem necessary for the benefit and usefulness of said canal; &c. * * * The members of the said Board of Control shall each receive such compensation for necessary services in going to and from, and inspecting such canal as shall be allowed by the Board of Auditors of this State, not exceeding the milage and per diem now paid members of the Legislature of this State," &c., and the first section of this act designates the Governor, Auditor General and Treasurer as the persons who shall constitute such Board of Control.

Thus it will be seen that this allowance is distinctly and expressly authorized by law, and instead of having been paid from the State Treasury it was paid out of the "Canal Fund," which is a separate and distinct fund, created expressly to defray the expenses of operating said canal, and appropriable to no other purposes.

In this connection we desire to mention but one more of the *item* alluded to in the "minority report," as follows:

"Another claim of $50, for the translation of the Governor's Message into the Chippewa language, was of no material utility, as not a single copy of said translation has ever come to light, and not one has ever reached those localities in the northern portions of the State, where those messages were intended to be distributed."

In introducing this item we do not intend to justify the necessity of it, but only to say that the translation was ordered by the Legislature upon the motion, and at the urgent solicitation of Hon. Abner Sherman, the Democratic member from the Chippewa country; that it was made and printed, and a copy of it is now in possession of the writer of this article. Had we any desire to establish the usefulness of this translation, we might probably compare it to a translation made by "the undersigned" himself in 1853, of the message of a Democratic Governor, the records and vouchers for which are now on file in the State Department, which we copy, as follows, "for the sole and only proper use, benefit and behoof" of "the undersigned."

"STATE OF MICHIGAN,
1853. TO EDWARD KANTER, DR.
Jan'y. For translation of the Governor's Annual
Message into the German Language, $75 00"

This "voucher" is endorsed as follows:

"Allowed and paid at $50 00, *Feb.* 11*th*, 1853."

But it seems this translation was incorrect, and useless, for in the same bundle of vouchers we find another, which reads as follows:

"STATE OF MICHIGAN,
1853. TO DR. RULOLPH, DR.
Jan. For *re-translation of Mr. Kanter's translation of the Governor's Annual Message,* .... $40 00"

which is endorsed,—"*allowed and paid Feb.* 11*th*, 1853"—being the same day on which Mr. Kanter's *original* translation was allowed and paid.

This "Dr. Rudolph" was at the date of the above interesting documents the proprietor of a Democratic German paper in the city of Detroit, and was allowed for "composition" on this same message at the rate of $1 76 per one thousand ems; or more than double the usual price! While "the undersigned" was pursuing his investigation, it would have been quite as well to have given the public some light in reference to the above transactions as to have confined his investigations to the propriety or usefulness of the "Chippewa translation." Perhaps, also, he might be induced to employ some competent person to correct the blunders in his "minority report," though we shall insist, (from personal experience,) that the sum paid for the job be something more than forty dollars!

In reference to the general policy of the large appropriations to the public works of the State by the Legislatures of 1855 and 1857, we think there can be no doubt. The people uniformly, and almost unanimously, approve them. It is known that when the Republicans came into power a large and expensive class of public and charitable institutions were upon their hands, none of which were completed, and but two of which were in operation. These public works were the offspring of Democratic policy, and although we heartily commend the objects of their establishment, and believe their speedy completion to be necessary to the general good and credit of the State, yet we cannot but regret that they were founded and begun in dimensions and at an ultimate cost far beyond any necessity, as well as the present ability of the State to complete. In founding these institutions, the same reckless and untempered spirit of extravagance which actuated and pervaded the Democratic party in contracting the old "Five Million Loan," and entering upon a gigantic scheme of internal improvement, was fostered, and all the dictates of caution and prudence pushed aside, that free scope might be given to the greedy ambition of the "camp followers" and speculators of the party. It was a question, not of policy, but of economy with the Republicans, whether they should make a concentrated and successful effort for the final completion of these immense works, thus thrown upon their hands, or allow them to drag along, unfinished, untenanted, practically useless to the State and to the objects contemplated in their commencement. If they have erred in these appropriations, it is simply an error in judgment, to which all men are liable; but even this cannot be conceded.

It is a well known fact, that when the Republicans came into power, all the public buildings were in a ruinous and dilapidated state. The Asylum for the Deaf and Dumb and Blind was an old wooden tenement, destitute of decent accommodations and many of the absolute necessary conveniences for its successful operation. The State Prison was minus largely in the necessary number of cells; its roofs were rotten and ready to tumble down; it had no dining-rooms, hospitals, solitary cells, or female departments, but was a conglomerated mass of reeking filth, disease, and ruins. The Insane Asylum at Kalamazoo presented only a huge pile of unfinished, uncovered walls; the meagre appropriations made by the Democratic Legislature for each year, hardly sufficing to repair the damaging effects of each succeeding winter, with no hope or prospect of ultimate completion or usefulness. Such were the inducements and circumstances that impelled the Republicans to increase their appropriations in the hope of putting all these institutions into successful and speedy operation, and effecting an ultimate saving of thousands, perhaps millions, of the people's money—a result which, with the single exception of the Insane Asylum, has been already accomplished.

It is not at all remarkable that "the undersigned," after making the condemnation of the attempt of the Republican administration to complete, enlarge and carry out the designs of our public works and charitable institutions one of his strong points, should attempt to find fault with the management and expenditures of each.

Beginning with the State Prison, "the undersigned" says:

"A comparative statement in the expenses for the support of the State Prison, show an aggregate of about $26,000 for any three years during the Democratic administration, while the expenditure for 1857, charged in the General Fund account for that purpose, is $25,000 for that single year, with an additional estimate of $25,000 for 1858. This three-fold increase on the expenditure of any year prior to 1855, is so much more noticeable, when we consider the greatly enhanced prices obtained for manual labor of the convicts, which had increased during the last three years from 31 to 56 cents per day, thereby making a difference in favor of the State of about $14,000 per annum, which, by a prudent economical management, should have made it long ago, a self-paying institution."

The peculiar, unparalleled and unwarranted fatality which pertains to the former figures of "the undersigned" is also manifest here. A comparison of the reports and expenses of the prison for the years 1852–3 and 4, show an aggregate expenditure over and above all receipts of $31,000 instead of $26,000, as asserted by the "report," being a difference of only $5,000. And in regard to the increased average expenditures of the State Prison, a comparison of the reports of different and successive years will show that this increase is considerably below the ratio of the increase of the number of inmates, and the varying prices of provisions and other expenses for the maintenance of the convicts. That we may arrive more definitely at the facts in the case, we propose to contrast a few figures showing the increased demands upon, as well as expenses of the institution:

By the report of the Inspectors for 1854, we find that there were in the Prison on the 30th day of December of that year,....................................246 convicts.
Nov. 30, 1857, there were in prison,.........411 "

Increase in 1857,.....................165 "

The daily average number of convicts in the prison during the year 1857, was......................378.8-10ths.
Daily average number for 1854,..............219.1-10th.

Increase,..............................159.7-10ths.

When we take into account this large increase in the number of convicts, the increased price of provisions during the last three years, over the three preceding, and the fact that, on an average, 135 of this number have been

employed by the State, upon the new building, in the yard, making clothes for convicts, cooking, in the female and solitary departments, and in the hospital, and of course from whose labor no direct revenue was derived, this increase is readily and properly accounted for. In 1854, the total number thus employed, and who produced no revenue, was only thirty-four. With this small number of convicts, nearly all of whom were employed upon contracts at the same rates received during nearly the whole of last year, with flour, meat and vegetables at least one-fourth cheaper, with a less number of guards and other officers, the expenses in 1854 amounted to $29,133 89. In 1857, with almost double the amount of prisoners, over one-third of whom produced no revenue, but were a direct tax upon the State, a larger number of officers, and greatly enhanced prices for provisions, the total expenses of the prison were only $50,203 16
From this deduct amount due from contractors, 9,562 78

Leaving the actual cost of operating and maintaining the Institution at............ ......$40,640 38

Being an increase in the expenses of maintaining that Institution in 1857, over 1854, of *less than one-third*, instead of, as "the undersigned" asserts, a "*three-fold*" increase of its expenditures.

It is also proper to remark here in regard to the "greatly enhanced prices obtained for manual labor of convicts," which, it is asserted, has "increased during the last three years from 31 to 56 cents per day," is a perversion of the facts in the case—as at the time of making the annual report of the Prison, Nov. 30th, 1857—but one of the new contracts had been entered into—that for constructing wagons, &c.,—which went into effect on the 1st of June previous—the others taking effect in the month of December last; and one, the "tool contract"—by far the largest in the Prison—not taking effect until the first of May next. It was undoubtedly the intention of "the undersigned" to deceive the people in reference to these facts, as he has evidently attempted to do in all his other statements and figures.

The same desperate fatality pervades the statements of "the undersigned" relative to the House of Correction. He says:

"I find, upon investigation, that, including the amount obtained for manual labor of the convicts, nearly $19,000 have been consumed by that institution during the last year, to support an average of thirty boys and girls—being an average expense of nearly $650 per annum for each of the inmates. The details of their expense for clothing, shoes, provisions, &c., will at a glance account for the high figures of the aggregate expense."

The annual report of the Board of Control of the House of Correction, shows the whole amount of expenditures made by said Board during the year 1857, to have been $12,923 74, instead of $19,000 00, as the "report" asserts; showing a variation from the facts of $6,076 26. Of this sum of $12,923 74, the official report of the Board shows the actual cost of maintainance of the inmates to have been,.................................. $6,376 98
Amount earned by inmates during the year,.... 468 05

Showing balance drawn from the Treasury,. $5,998 93

Which divided by 30, the average number of inmates, gives as the cost to the State of the maintenance of each, the sum of $196 96¼, instead of $650 each, as is asserted by "the undersigned." The balance of the whole amount expended was appropriated to building purposes, improvements, repairs, &c., and is not, in any proper light to be charged into the cost of maintaining the inmates of the institution.

In this connection "the undersigned" insinuates some flagrant wrong-doing in the allowance to Whitney Jones, Auditor General, in the settlement of his claim for land used for the site of the House of Correction. In this matter his version is partly true, as Mr. Jones was allowed $600 for his premises used therefor; but vouchers on file show that in arranging the site for the buildings, it was necessary that some other lands should be purchased, and at the urgent solicitation of citizens of Lansing, Colonel Jones obligated himself to pay a considerable larger sum than that allowed by the Board. After re-deeding the land to the State, or so much as was needed, Col. Jones was paid a fair and just equivalent for the lands used, the remaining portion of which he now owns or is obliged to pay for. A full record of the whole transaction appears upon the books of the Auditor, a reference to which would have saved "the undersigned" the necessity of this foul and unprovoked attack upon a candid and faithful public officer; one to whom "the undersigned" has frequently acknowledged himself indebted for favors, and whom he has often alluded to as a high-minded and courteous gentleman—a distinction we fear "the undersigned," in view of these assertions, cannot claim.

The attack upon the Agricultural College comes with bad grace from a member of a party which incorporated into the Constitution of the State, a provision requiring its erection. In reference to it, we can only say that it was undertaken as *an experiment;* and that having proven itself useful and successful, other States are now preparing to follow the example we have set them, by forming similar institutions. As to its cost, when compared with the difficulties to be overcome, it has been founded, put into operation, and achieved a reputation as a successful and useful educational institution, at a less expense than any other College of like capacities, extent and conveniences, in the world.

The next position which we shall notice is relative to the "comparative statement of the assessment of State taxes." Upon this head "the undersigned" very complacently says, such a comparison "can hardly be arrived at with any certainty and correctness," and the remark is a just one, as his previous abortive attempts at figuring have undoubtedly convinced the reader. The statement of the "report," that the State tax suddenly fell off from an annual average of $116,579, for the years 1848, '49, '50, '51, and '52, to only $10,000 in 1853, and was only $30,000 in 1854, making "only $40,000 taxation for two years," will undoubtedly excite some surprise on the part of those who have not given the subject a full examination. These figures alone would imply that the "Democratic" administration had suddenly so economized the expenses of our government that taxation would have been entirely done away with, if it could have been permitted to hold the reins another term. Aye, more. Another two years, with a like economical stride, there would have been a surplus of receipts, with no taxation whatever, to distribute among the people! But the truth is, the expenses of government were about the same as they were in previous years; and at the same time, our "State institutions" were suffered to decay for the want of necessary repairs.

But where did the money come from to pay the expenses of government? The records furnish an answer to this question. The Trust Funds were resorted to, and expended.

To overthrow the sophistry, the quibbling attempt to dodge the whole truth of the question by "the undersigned," we can do no better than to quote a few paragraphs from the majority report, as follows:

Comparative Statement of State Tax, from 1848 to 1857, inclusive—10 years.

YEAR	Valuation	Tax.	Per cent in mills.
1848, ...	$ 29,908,769 00	$150,719 00	5.04
1849, ...	28,999,202 00	102,406 00	3.53
1850, ...	29,384,270 00	113,768 00	3.87
1851, ...	30,976,270 00	106,000 00	3.42
1852, ...	30,976,270 00	110,000 00	3.55
1853, ...	120,362,474 00	10,000 00	0.08
1854, ...	120,362,474 00	30,000 00	0.25
Total, ...	$390,969,729 00	$622,892 00	1.59
1855, ...	$120,362,474 00	$40,000 00	0.33
1856, ...	137,663,009 00	65,000 00	0.47
1857, ...	137,663,009 00	85,000 00	0.61
Total, ...	$395,688,492 00	$190,000 00	0.47

Average valuation, for first seven years,.......$55,852,818
" State tax, per year,................ 89,984
" rate per cent., or mills per dollar, 1½ mills.

For the second period of three years:
Average valuation for three years,..........$131,896,164
" State tax per year,................ 63,335
" rate per cent., or mills per dollar, 47-100 of a mill.

During the first period of seven years, from 1848 to 1854, inclusive, the total valuation of property for the whole period, was..................................$390,969,929
The total amount of State tax assessed,...... 622,892
And the average rate per dollar, 1½ mills.

During the first three years of the present administration, the total assessed value of property in the State was..................................$395,688,492
Total amount of State tax,................ 190,065
The average rate per cent., 47-100 of a mill.

Showing an average annual tax of $25,529 less than during the former period; and that upon a valuation of $96,043,346 greater—being a difference of *over one hundred per cent.* in the rate of taxation in favor of the present administration.

These facts and figures were equally accessable to the majority and minority, and had "the undersigned" really wished to make any comparisons, they might have been made as above, with the most absolute "certainty and correctness."

Leaving the point of taxation, "the undersigned" turns his attention to the State debt, and sets up the absurd and grotesque plea that during the last seven years of its rule the Democratic administrations reduced the State debt a total of $254,012 62; that is to say, they had paid that amount of outstanding bonds, over and above all contingencies, and interest, making an absolute reduction of the debt to that amount.

A cursory glance at the public records would seem to substantiate this statement; but a more close examination will establish its entire falsity. Instead of decreasing the State debt between the years 1847 and 1854, the State indebtedness was *increased over half a million of dollars.* However astonishing this fact may appear, it is beyond the power of successful contradiction.

In 1854, Auditor General Swegles, in his report dated Nov. 30th of that year, gives as the total funded and fundable debt of the State the sum of..........$2,531,545 70

Auditor General D. V. Bell, in his report dated Dec. 1st, 1847, gives as the "total debt of the State for which she is liable, without contingency,"...........................	2,290,768 51
Which figures show *an actual increase of the State indebtedness*, from 1847 to 1854, *under Democratic administrations of*.............	$240,777 19
Add to this the sums appropriated for the use of the State from the Trust Funds up to that date,.............................	676,288 80
Thus making an increase of the general fund indebtedness in the last seven years of Democratic rule of..........................	$917,065 99
Deduct from this for bonds surrendered and canceled in 1852, '53 and '54,.............	254,012 62
And we have as the *actual* increase of this class of debt, under these economical Democratic administrations, the sum of..........	$663,053 37

And yet, in the face and eyes of these plain and palpable figures, this "report" says, to which result of its financiering, "the Democratic party have a right to look with pride." Its pride is easily flattered in these days. These results, added to the developments relating to the absorption and expenditures of the Trust Funds, shown up in the former part of this article, certainly entitle the Democratic party to *credit*, if it is not flattering to their pride.

The attempt of "the undersigned" to give a "statement of the cash receipts and disbursements from Nov. 30th to Jan. 26th," "is a singular one," indeed. His constant perversion of facts and the plainest figures; such unmitigated and wilful lying and deceit are tiresome, we know, to the reader, and for fear of wearing your patience, we shall be as brief as possible upon this point. The "report" says:

"The statement of cash receipts and disbursements from November 30 to January 26, as furnished to the undersigned by the Deputy Treasurer, is a singular one—*all expenditures*, and hardly any receipts."

By referring to the statement of the Treasurer as embodied in the majority report, we find the statement to stand thus:

Expenditures,	$29,157 46
Receipts,	19,158 67
Excess of expenditures,	$9,268 79

The "report" continues:

"That a portion of the $117,105 73, *which is claimed* to have been expended since November 30, has been paid before the end of the fiscal year 1857, there is in the mind of the undersigned no room for doubt, and was probably kept out of the former account to make a good show at the end of the fiscal year."

Neither the report of the majority or the statement of the Treasurer *claimed* that any such sum had been expended as is here represented. Now look at the figures of "the undersigned." He says the amount expended from November 30 to January 26, was $117,105 73

Actual amount expended,	29,157 46
Variation of "the undersigned" from facts,	$88,048 27

The reader can place the proper estimate upon the intention of "the undersigned" in making this statement. But he proceeds:

"How can it be otherwise, when the undersigned discovers among the disbursements during the short period of fifty-seven days, salaries for State officers, $8,000, vouchers for warrants, $8,000, redemption certificates, $5,000," &c.

This wonder is easily accounted for by the fact that the salaries fall due, and these balances are always settled upon the 1st day of January; and hence could not be incorporated into a report made on the 30th of November preceding. The "report" continues:

"As to the receipts since November 30, the undersigned

is astonished at the smallness of the figures, the gross receipts being only $19,158 67, of which $12,000 were lately paid by the Detroit and Milwaukee Railroad for specific taxes; leaving only $7,158 67 for nearly two months income from all other quarters. This looks almost like an improbability."

Yes, and it *is an improbability*, as the sum of $12,000 *had not been paid* by the D. & M. R. R. for specific taxes. True, $10,000 *had been deposited with the Treasurer*, but no credit had been given on the books of the office, nor could it be done until the whole sum was paid. So instead of the current receipts having been *only* $7,157 67, they were just $19,158 67, to which add the specific tax mentioned *and due*, and the sum would have been 31,158 67, or over $2,000 more than the current expenses for the same period. Perhaps it is not improper to state, that while large drafts are annually made upon the Treasury in the months of January and February, for the payment of interest, expenses of the Legislature, salaries, &c., full one-half of the total receipts in the Treasury accrue in the months of March, April and May; thus, while the expenditures always show an excess during the winter months, the receipts always show an excess in the spring and fall months; thus is explained that marvelous and incomprehensible wonder, which seems to have so greatly exercised "the undersigned" in this particular.

We have now fully met and refuted every charge of the "report" against the Republican party and the present administration—have, by a fair, honest and truthful exhibit of *official and indisputable* figures disproved every assertion of extravagance made therein—have by unimpeachable testimony convicted "the undersigned" of most wilful and unqualified perversion of facts and figures—have exhibited the unparalleled recklessness and extravagance of every position and assertion, and fully shown up the despicable and lying character of this pretended "report." The reader is already convinced of its utter want of candor, reliability, or even decency. Here, perhaps, it would be proper for us to close our review, but in justice to the Republican party, and in the hope that no reader is so bigoted as to refuse us a full hearing, we will venture to criticise, and enlarge somewhat upon the concluding portions of the "report," and such other facts as we may deem intimately connected therewith.

Firstly, in this connection, we shall notice some of the frauds committed on the Treasury by this Democratic party during the last days of its power, in answer to the *apologies* contained in the "minority report." That "the undersigned" should feel slightly distressed at the state of facts presented in the majority report relative to these frauds is not a matter of surprise. The unparalleled extravagance of the Democratic Board of Auditors, during the month of December, 1854, in allowing claims to the amount of $53,568 29 in a single month, and that, too, the last of their official life, *is* a matter to excite surprise; The "*dubious character*" of all these claims, including that of the Phœnix Bank, to Job Brookfield, Gilbert & Co., Bronson, Knight & Ingalls, and others; all claims that had been for years before the people and often rejected by the Legislature and by previous agents of the State, certainly demanded an *apology* at his hands. Hence, the "report" says:

"In reference to the charges made against the last Democratic Board of State Auditors, during the last thirty days of their existence, the undersigned would observe that the action upon the claims allowed on the old Internal Improvement contracts, have never been defended by the Democratic party, by resolution, or by the support of its press."

Fully believing in the triteness of the old saying that one should "never spoil a good story for relations sake," we simply desire to call the attention of "the undersigned" to the fact that these same men are still classed among the leading, influential men of his party, and that while his party press *have not dared to defend these allowances*, it has uniformly sought to ridicule and defeat any attempt of the present Administration to recover any portion of this enormous plunder. Of the truth of this assertion let the course of the Detroit *Free Press* and the remarks of "the undersigned" himself, referring to the Phœnix Bank case, bear testimony.

But these allowances are not alone a monument to the knavery and dishonesty of the Democratic party. During this same month of December, other and more monstrous allowances and expenses were made by this pure party "the undersigned" so humbly apologies for. We subjoin some of the items, as follows: salaries, $2,997 87; extra clerks, one month, $791 37; fitting up the Legislative Halls, $2,717 27; *Legislative* printing and publishing laws (twenty months after the Legislature had adjourned,) $2,841 07; stationery to Auditor General, $674 55; printing paper, $651; to commissioner of fire-proof offices, $782; improvements on Capitol Square, (which square "the undersigned" was unable to find,) $3,406 13; postage, $427 61, or at the rate of over five thousand dollars per year!! uncurrent funds, $458 55!! and other like items, swelling the whole amount of such expenditures to the sum of $83,-962 71, or costing the State, in the month of December, 1854, alone, only $4,682 52 less than for the whole year previous. Is it any wonder that this benighted and afflicted representative of an unscrupulous and defunct Democracy, should attempt to *apologise* for such bare-faced frauds and peculations, or that his apology is *very lame?*

"The undersigned" does not even so much as attempt an *apology* for the double allowance to Hon. Geo. W. Peck, (and with this we should find serious fault did we not know that gentleman had the supervision of the whole report,) State Printer, nor to the Timber Stealer Fox, nor for the defalcations of *St. John* Swegles. He pleads *convenient ignorance* in these matters, and tries to slide out by the *simple* remark that *those individuals* alone must bear the responsibility—truly a new method of escaping the consequences of political dishonesty.

Upon the point of the origin of the State indebtedness, "the undersigued" says he "deems it sufficient to quote a single paragraph from the first message of the present Executive." Perhaps this *is* satisfactory to him—it is not at all unsatisfactory to us—yet we deem it of some trifling interest to investigate a fact or two not there stated. That the negotiation of the "five million loan" was "prompted by a wild spirit of excitement and speculation; that by it "an immense debt was created;" that our "gigantic system of internal improvements" yielded "little or no revenue," and as a natural consequence "the State was soon brought to the verge of bankruptcy and ruin," are all facts which no one will deny; but the mere recital of these facts will not in the least relieve the Democratic party from the responsibility it incurred in yielding to the temptation, and thus burdening the State, in its infancy, with this debt and its still enduring legacy of interest and taxation.

From the first inception of our State indebtedness to the close of the Democratic reign in 1854, was one continual chain of monstrous frauds and reckless trifling with the interests of the people. We have prepared the following figures only as a sample of the management during the "iron rule of the Democracy."

The amount of Bonds issued, May, 1838, was,	$5,200,000 00
Of which the State rec'd pay and in full, only,	1,387,000 00
Remaining unpaid,..................	$3,813,000 00

For which sum the then Democratic Administration took the Morris Canal Co. as security, and delivered the whole amount of bonds, and upon which the State received from said Company, previous to its failure, only $955,960 24. Showing in this transaction a loss to the State of *only* $2,857,039 76, upon the original bonds for the "five million loan." Instead of promptly adjusting these Bonds and paying the interest upon them annually, the Democratic Administration, after disgracing the State with an insane attempt at repudiation, allowed this indebtedness and the accumulating interest to remain unsettled and unpaid during their continuance in power, and it was not until the present Republican Administration came into power, that a law was passed requiring the prompt surrender of the Bonds, and by cutting off the accumulation of interest, secured their adjustment. Up to the 1st of January, 1858, the total amount of indebtedness thus adjusted by the Republicans, including the interest which had accrued under the Democratic regime, was..........$1,809,395 73

Amount still outstanding, Jan. 1, 1858,......	113.399 .72
Making the present indebtedness on the five million loan,........................	$1,922,795 45
Deduct from this the original debt,.........	955,960 24
And you have the sum of...........	$966,835 21

Or $10,874 97 more than the original indebtedness as the accumulation of interest during the rule of the Democracy, and showing a dead loss to the people of the State of

On account of the principal,................	$2,857,039 76
On the interest,..........................	966,835 21
Or a total loss of..................	$3,823,874 97

Besides the sums unknown, for exchange, expenses, &c., upon the five million loan alone. And yet in the face of such figures as these, this "report" eulogizes those Democratic Administrations, and says the people "understand too well the faithfulness with which the public interests were consulted in all measures of State policy, to require any defence before them of *those* administrations."

Well may "the undersigned" close his "report" with the

jubilant assertion that "the people have *too often* and *too emphatically* endorsed the Administrations of Gov. Barry and Gov. Felch." Yes, indeed! the people have realized the truth of that saying, and in the last campaign gave them each an equally *emphatic* endorsement, after a full knowledge of the facts—by leaving Gov. Barry in a *minority* of *six thousand votes* in his Congressional District, and by refusing, by a majority of near *twenty thousand votes* to again entrust the management of our State finances to the hands of Gov. Felch! *Emphatic endorsement, indeed!!* And this same people, with a more full understanding of all these facts, and after sifting the silly falsehoods of the "minority report," are now waiting impatiently to record another and a like *endorsement,* only more withering and annihilating, of the financial policy of this Democratic party. Yes, "*too* often"—altogether too often did they embrace its *swindling extravagance* and *irresponsible demagogues;* and now that the facts are before them, and they are reaping the full fruition of that dishonest and disastrous policy, their future *endorsement* will be like the last—*utter condemnation.*

www.ingramcontent.com/pod-product-compliance
Lightning Source LLC
LaVergne TN
LVHW011139110826
845150LV00008B/2411
9781418193256